kid chef junior bakes

kid chef junior BAKES

MY *First* KIDS' BAKING COOKBOOK

Charity Mathews

FOUNDER OF FOODLETS.COM

PHOTOGRAPHY BY MARIJA VIDAL

ROCKRIDGE PRESS

For my family of bakers big and small, Violet, George, Estelle, Phoebe, and Paul.

CONTENTS

A NOTE TO GROWN-UPS

As a mom of four small kids, my best advice about baking with little ones is simple: Don't underestimate them. Children can do so much more than you think!

I've been cooking with my kids since my oldest was a toddler, perched on a kitchen stool in our apartment in Rome. She tackled easy jobs that gave her confidence: pulling tomatoes off their stems, rubbing olive oil on sliced potatoes whose next stop was a hot oven. Dressed up in a miniature apron, she took her jobs pretty seriously for someone who wasn't even old enough to ride a bike. Gradually I gave her more complicated tasks and, little by little, her skills and her can-do attitude grew. This spring, for Mother's Day, that same kid produced a double-chocolate layer cake in the shape of a heart topped with fluffy meringue frosting. She also turned 10.

Now we live in North Carolina and the rest of my brood cooks, too. Every Sunday night a different kid cooks dinner, complete with dessert. With all those kids cooking, you can bet we tested every one of the recipes in this book. Cooking teaches kids about the time and effort it takes to cook food and how the results are so much tastier and fresher than anything you'd ever buy at the store. Plus, it's a life skill they'll always be grateful to have.

There's another lesson, too. Cooking requires patience, curiosity, and gumption. Once our kids started finding themselves in the hot seat, they found more gratitude and polite words for other cooks on other nights. Win, win. All the wins.

The recipes in this book are simplified versions of my family's favorite baked goods, from biscuits to cake. Each recipe is marked easy, medium, or hard. Easy recipes can be done by kids with very little help. You won't see a lot of chopping or using a hot stove there. Hard recipes require more teamwork with a grown-up. It's simple to divide any recipe between kids and grown-ups: grown-ups take the tasks marked with a (STOP) and kids can generally do the rest.

To start, let your kids flip through the book with a stack of Post-it notes, marking the dishes that they want to bake first. Then, find an easy recipe to begin with. Read through the recipe aloud together so you know what to expect. Confirm whether you have the ingredients and kitchen tools on hand. Pick a time to bake and tell your child about the plan. Speaking from experience, there's nothing quite like a kid who wants to start "right now!" so this time frame is key.

In Chapter 1, "A Kid's Kitchen," you'll find tips on kid-safe kitchen equipment and handy kitchen rules that I've used for years. But you know your child best, so use your own judgment on where to set limits.

Here are a few more tried-and-true tips that work for baking with my own crew:

- Make having fun the goal. Baking with kids isn't about pin-worthy results (or a speedy finish—see below). When I've got kiddos in the kitchen, I try to reset my expectations, aimed at one thing: building them up. I want to teach them a few skills and make them feel good about the process. If they want to cook together again when we're done, that's a victory.

- Allow plenty of time. Baking with kids takes much longer than whipping up a cobbler on your own. To help speed things up, read through the recipe ahead of time and set out your ingredients and kitchen tools. You'll find things go more smoothly.

- Set timing expectations. On that note, be sure kids understand if a recipe has a start-and-stop rhythm. Many doughs need to rise, chill, or rest, and every recipe needs to bake and cool.

- Have a wet rag on hand. Sticky fingers and spills are coming.

- Ditto for a garbage bowl. Racing back and forth to the trash can adds to the kitchen chaos.

- Read the Kitchen Rules (see page 2) with your child before starting. This sets the groundwork for everything from washing hands to cleaning as you go, without you having to be the heavy.

A NOTE TO KIDS

Welcome to the delicious world of baking!
With this book, you have all the information you
need to bake 25 of my own kids' favorite cookies,
cakes, muffins, and more—even pizza.

Whether you're new to baking or practically a
chef, this book is just for you. You'll find breakfast ideas, snacks, yummy lunches you can take
to school, and, of course, desserts. Each recipe
is rated easy, medium, or hard. Easy recipes are
dishes you can make almost entirely by yourself.
Harder recipes will require more help. Every time
you see a , that's your cue to ask a grown-up to
step in. Otherwise, the baking is up to you!

You can even write in this book. There's space to
make a note about each dish when you're done: the
date you baked it, who helped, and your star rating.
There are even some coloring pages at the back of
the book to decorate.

I hope you have as much fun baking these
recipes as my kids have. Now let's get started!

a kid's kitchen

Congratulations! You might not know it yet, but you're in for a treat—in more ways than one. Baking is a skill that you'll enjoy for the rest of your life. By starting as a kid, you've got a head start on years of cookies, cakes, pies, bagels, and biscuits to come. Are you hungry yet? Let's dig in.

KITCHEN RULES

A kitchen is a delicious place that can also be dangerous. There are three main ways a cooking session could go wrong: heat, blades, and food poisoning. But don't worry. By taking a few simple steps, you can stay safe, organized, and in the fun zone.

1. **Always cook with a grown-up.** These recipes are made for kids to enjoy, but you always need a grown-up to help. When you see a 🛑 symbol, that means stop and ask a grown-up to join you. Usually this is a step using the oven, food processor, hot water, or any task that could be dangerous to do on your own.

2. **Wash your hands.** Clean hands are the most useful tool in the kitchen! Before baking, always wash your hands with soap and warm water. But don't rush. Make sure your hands are truly clean, by singing the A-B-C song while you scrub. When the song's over, your hands should be ready to bake.

NOTE TO GROWN-UPS

Now is a good time to go over any specific rules you have in your kitchen that may not be mentioned here.

3. **Handle eggs safely.** Refrigerated eggs can be left on the counter for up to two hours before baking. Bringing them up to room temperature can help with baking. But you don't need to do that for any of the recipes in this book, so it's okay to skip. Always wash your hands after handling raw eggs.

4. **Use pot holders.** The oven is hot, hot, hot! It will burn your skin instantly (ditto for any pans coming out), so always ask a grown-up for a hand.

5. **Prepare your work area.** Before starting any baking project, set up all the ingredients on a clean, flat work space. Get your measuring cups and spoons ready, grab a bowl, and make sure the pan you need is handy. You'll save time—and disappointment—if you know you have everything you need from the start. You don't want to be halfway through a recipe only to find out you're missing a key ingredient.

6. **Clean as you go.** Keep a wet rag and a garbage bowl on the counter. Wipe up any spills as they happen and tidy your space between steps as needed. You'll save a lot of time when it comes to cleanup at the end.

BAKING EQUIPMENT

Just like an artist needs paint, a few key pieces of equipment can help beginning bakers succeed. Here are my favorites:

TOOLS & UTENSILS

Apple slicer	**Bread knife**	**Butter knife**	**Cookie scoop**
Cooling rack	**Cupcake liners**	**Cutting board**	**Grater**

Ice cream scoop

Kid-safe knives

Measuring cups

Measuring spoons

Paper towels

Parchment paper

Pastry brush

Pastry cutter (optional)

Pizza cutter

Plastic wrap

Potato masher (optional)

Rolling pin

Sifter

Silicone baking mats

Silicone spatula

Slotted spoon

Vegetable peeler

Whisk

Wooden mixing spoons (optional)

Zester

COOKWARE & BAKEWARE

Baking pan (8-by-8-inch, 9-by-9-inch, and 9-by-13-inch)

Baking sheet (two 9-by-13-inch)

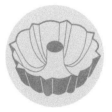

Bundt pan

Cake pan (8-inch and 9-inch [round])

Large pot (including 6- to 8-quart covered pot [cast iron, enamel, or ceramic])

Loaf pan (8½-by-4½-inch or 9-by-5-inch)

Microwave-safe bowls

Mixing bowls (small, medium, and large)

Muffin pan (two 12-cup)

Skillet (including cast iron)

APPLIANCES

Food processor

Stand mixer with paddle attachment and dough hook or electric beaters

BAKING CLASS

Baking is both an art and a science. Adding a few extra sprinkles here and there? Art. Measuring the exact amount of baking powder? That's science. You need both to get yummy results. Here's my best advice:

- **Read the recipe.** From start to finish. It tells you everything you'll need and everything you'll be doing. Picture yourself going through each step, and ask a grown-up if anything seems confusing before you start baking.

- **Make sure you have all the ingredients.** Set out all the ingredients you'll need. Not only is it handier to have it all ready when you need it, but if you're missing anything, you'll notice BEFORE you start baking.

- **Get out all the tools.** It's no fun to search for a spatula when you've got cookie dough all over your hands—and worse, when you realize there isn't a spatula available. Even experienced cooks have whipped up a cake batter only to discover their favorite cake pan is in the dishwasher, dirty.

- **Measure carefully.** Remember, baking is a science. Ingredients like baking powder and baking soda are called leavening agents—they make dough and batter rise! But be careful. Adding the wrong amounts can give your baked goods a terrible taste or texture. Use measuring cups for dry ingredients (like flour and sugar) and scrape off the top with the back of a butter knife. Wet ingredients should be measured in a glass measuring cup. Bend down so your eyes are even with the liquid: If the level of the liquid is even with the marks on the side of the cup, you've got the right amount.

- **Be stove and oven safe.** Always ask a grown-up to help with jobs around the oven or stove. Pot holders should be dry (wet pot holders allow heat to zip right through and burn you). Don't microwave anything with metal, and never microwave anything for longer than 30 seconds at a time.

Secret Ingredient
Double-Chocolate
Cookies page 16

cookies & bars

Giant cookies, gooey brownies, and even a cookie you can eat for breakfast! Plus, double-chocolate treats with a secret superfood ingredient, and coconut cookies that transform from an anytime treat to something special for holidays.

coconut macaroon mountains

With mounds of sweet coconut, this simplified classic is impossible not to love.

PREP TIME
65 minutes

COOK TIME
15 minutes

MAKES
30
COOKIES

EGG-FREE
NUT-FREE
VEGETARIAN

KITCHEN TOOLS YOU WILL NEED

Large mixing bowl

Measuring cups

Measuring spoons

Silicone spatula or wooden mixing spoon

2 9-by-13-inch baking sheets

Parchment paper or silicone baking mats

Cookie scoop or 2 spoons

INGREDIENTS YOU WILL NEED

14 ounces **sweetened condensed milk**

1 teaspoon **vanilla extract**

⅔ cup **flour**

5½ cups **sweetened coconut flakes** (14-ounce bag)

¼ teaspoon **salt**

DIRECTIONS

1. Mix the batter. In a large mixing bowl, use a silicone spatula or wooden mixing spoon to stir the sweetened condensed milk, vanilla, flour, coconut, and salt together until every piece of coconut is coated with the sweet mixture. To add the flour correctly, use a second measuring cup to spoon flour into the ⅔-cup measuring cup, flatten off the top, and pour the flour into the mixing bowl.

2. **Chill the batter.** Place the mixing bowl in the refrigerator for 1 hour.

3. **Bake the macaroons.** (STOP) Preheat the oven to 350°F. While it's warming up, line two baking sheets with parchment paper or silicone baking mats. Use a cookie scoop (or two spoons) to make 2-inch balls. Place each scoop on the baking sheets. (STOP) Bake for 15 minutes, until the edges look golden and crispy.

MAKE IT YOUR OWN

Macaroons are perfect for festive occasions:

For Spring: Add 1 tablespoon of cocoa powder when you're mixing the batter. Before baking, press your thumb down on the scooped batter to create an indent. When the macaroons cool, fill with jelly beans for adorable springtime bird nests!

Want to get really decadent? Dip the bottom of your macaroons in melted chocolate. Or get really cute by doing the same thing with colored candy melts!

secret ingredient double-chocolate cookies

The secret ingredient is avocado, which acts like butter in this recipe, making the cookies super fudgy.

PREP TIME
10 minutes

COOK TIME
10 minutes

MAKES
12
COOKIES

NUT-FREE
VEGETARIAN

KITCHEN TOOLS YOU WILL NEED

9-by-13-inch baking sheet

Parchment paper or silicone baking mat

Cutting board

Kid-safe knife

Spoon

Large mixing bowl

Fork or potato masher

Measuring cups

Silicone spatula or wooden mixing spoon

Measuring spoons

Medium mixing bowl

Ice cream scoop

INGREDIENTS YOU WILL NEED

1 ripe **avocado**

½ cup **sugar**

1 **egg**

½ cup **cocoa powder**

½ cup **flour**

½ teaspoon **baking soda**

½ cup **chocolate chips**

DIRECTIONS

1. Preheat the oven and prepare the pan. 🛑
Preheat the oven to 350°F. While it's warming up, line a 9-by-13-inch baking sheet with parchment paper or a silicone baking mat.

2. Peel and mash the avocado. On a cutting board with a kid-safe knife, cut the avocado in half lengthwise. Use a spoon to pop out the pit and scoop out the insides. Place the peeled avocado in a large mixing bowl. Use a fork or potato masher to mash your avocado into a paste.

3. **Mix the sugar and add the egg.** Add the sugar to the avocado and stir with a silicone spatula or wooden mixing spoon until combined. In a medium bowl, crack 1 egg. Remove any shell and pour the egg into the large bowl with the sugar and avocado. Mix well.

4. **Add the dry ingredients.** Add the cocoa powder, flour, baking soda, and chocolate chips to the wet ingredients. To add the flour correctly, use a second measuring cup to spoon flour into the ½-cup measuring cup, flatten off the top, and pour the flour into the mixing bowl. Stir well until you can't see any flour, about 10 to 15 times. The mixture will look dry.

5. **Bake the cookies.** Use an ice cream scoop to measure out the batter and place each scoop on the baking sheet. 🛑 Bake for 10 minutes. Allow to cool before serving.

world's biggest chocolate chip cookie

The only thing more fun than baking a batch of chocolate chip cookies is whipping up one giant cookie—stuffed with every type of chip you can think of!

PREP TIME
20 minutes

COOK TIME
40 minutes

MAKES
8 TO 10
SERVINGS

NUT-FREE
VEGETARIAN

KITCHEN TOOLS YOU WILL NEED

Paper towel

Cast iron skillet or round pie pan

Stand mixer or large mixing bowl with electric beaters

Measuring cups

Silicone spatula

Medium mixing bowl

Measuring spoons

Softened: Take your butter out of the refrigerator 30 minutes before you start baking to make sure it is soft.

INGREDIENTS YOU WILL NEED

1 tablespoon **butter**, plus 1 cup (2 sticks), softened*

1 cup **brown sugar**, packed

½ cup **granulated sugar**

2 **eggs**

1 tablespoon **vanilla extract**

2½ cups **all-purpose flour**

1 teaspoon **baking soda**

½ teaspoon **salt**

½ cup **chocolate chips** (keep about 12 for smiley face)

½ cup **butterscotch chips**

½ cup **white chocolate chips**

½ cup **toffee bits**

I MADE THIS
RECIPE ON:
(DATE)

- -

IT TASTED:
(CIRCLE
THE STARS)

★ ★ ★ ★ ★

WHO
HELPED?

- -

- -

- -

JUST FOR
LAUGHS

Why didn't Cookie Monster make his bed?

He couldn't find cookie sheets!

DIRECTIONS

1. Preheat the oven and prepare the pan. 🛑
Preheat the oven to 350°F. Use a paper towel with 1 tablespoon of softened butter to grease a cast iron skillet or round pie pan.

2. Cream* **the sugars.** In a stand mixer or large mixing bowl with electric beaters, beat the butter, brown sugar, and granulated sugar together until whipped, about 2 minutes. Use a silicone spatula to scrape down the edges of the bowl.

Cream: Whip butter together with sugar until fluffy.

3. Add the wet ingredients. In a medium bowl, crack 1 egg. Remove any shell and pour the egg into the large bowl. Repeat with the second egg. Add the vanilla and beat again, about 2 minutes.

4. Add the dry ingredients. To add the flour correctly, use a second measuring cup to spoon flour into the 1-cup measuring cup, flatten off the top, pour the flour into the mixing bowl, and repeat. Repeat once more with the ½-cup measuring cup. Add the baking soda and salt. Beat on low until just mixed, about 15 seconds.

5. Pour in the chips. Add the chocolate chips (except for 12), butterscotch chips, white chocolate chips, and toffee bits. Use the spatula to combine evenly.

6. Bake. Transfer the batter to the buttered skillet. Use clean hands to smooth out the batter in the skillet. Add chocolate chips in the shape of a happy face. 🛑 Bake for 40 minutes.

? DID YOU KNOW?

Sugar used to be so rare and precious that only kings and queens could afford it.

best-morning-ever breakfast cookies 🧤🧤

With a swirl of sweet cinnamon, cranberries, and toasted oats, this cookie is good for you—and delicious with a glass of milk.

PREP TIME
10 minutes
COOK TIME
25 minutes

MAKES
8 OR 9
COOKIES

EGG-FREE
VEGETARIAN

KITCHEN TOOLS YOU WILL NEED

9-by-13-inch baking sheet

Parchment paper

Large mixing bowl or stand mixer

Fork or potato masher

Measuring cups

Measuring spoons

Silicone spatula

Ice cream scoop

INGREDIENTS YOU WILL NEED

Nonstick cooking spray, for greasing the pan (optional)

1 large **banana**, mashed (or 2 small bananas)

3 tablespoons **butter**, melted

3 tablespoons **honey**

2 tablespoons **milk**

1 cup **old-fashioned oats**

½ cup **whole wheat flour**

½ cup **dried cranberries**

½ cup **unsalted pumpkin seeds**

¼ cup **ground flaxseed** (or an extra ¼ cup flour)

1 tablespoon **chia seeds** (optional)

1 teaspoon ground **cinnamon**

½ teaspoon **baking powder**

¼ teaspoon **salt**

DIRECTIONS

1. Preheat the oven and prepare the pan. 🛑 Preheat your oven to 350°F. Line a baking sheet with parchment paper or coat with nonstick cooking spray.

2. Measure and stir together the wet ingredients. In a large mixing bowl, use a fork or potato masher to smash the banana. (If using a mixer, add the banana and mix on high for 20 seconds.) Add the melted butter, honey, and milk. Stir with a silicone spatula until well blended.

3. Measure the dry ingredients, and mix all the ingredients. Add the oats, flour, dried cranberries, pumpkin seeds, ground flaxseed (or extra flour), chia seeds (if using), cinnamon, baking powder, and salt. To add the

flour correctly, use a second measuring cup to spoon flour into the ½-cup measuring cup, flatten off the top, and pour the flour into the mixing bowl. Stir well. Let sit for about 5 minutes while the chia and flax seeds puff up.

4. **Bake the breakfast cookies.** Use an ice cream scoop to measure the batter and place each scoop onto the baking sheet. Use clean palms or the back of a spoon to gently press down, slightly flattening out the dough to a thick cookie shape. 🛑 Bake in the oven for 25 minutes, until the breakfast cookies are golden around the edges. Store in an airtight container for 2 to 3 days.

MAKE IT YOUR OWN

No cranberries or pumpkin seeds? Substitute any combination of nuts, seeds, and dried fruit or chocolate chips.

I MADE IT MY OWN BY:

....

....

....

....

....

....

? DID YOU KNOW?

Whole oats are a superfood, full of compounds called antioxidants that help keep our bodies healthy.

4-ingredient hazelnut brownies

Gooey in the center with a crackly top, these brownies are so perfect you'll never guess that you only need four ingredients to make them.

PREP TIME
5 minutes
COOK TIME
25 minutes

MAKES
9
BROWNIES

VEGETARIAN

KITCHEN TOOLS YOU WILL NEED

8-by-8-inch baking pan

Parchment paper

Large mixing bowl

Measuring cups

Measuring spoons

Silicone spatula

Cutting board

Kid-safe knife

INGREDIENTS YOU WILL NEED

2 **eggs**

1 13-ounce jar **hazelnut-chocolate spread** (about 1½ cups)

½ cup **all-purpose flour**

¼ teaspoon **salt**

DIRECTIONS

1. Preheat the oven and prepare the pan. (STOP)
Preheat the oven to 350°F. Line an 8-by-8-inch baking pan with parchment paper, extending the paper over the edges. (After baking, you'll use the paper as a handle to remove your brownies from the pan.)

2. Measure and stir together the ingredients. In a large mixing bowl, crack 1 egg and remove any shell. Repeat with the second egg. Add the hazelnut-chocolate spread, flour, and salt. To add the flour correctly, use a second

measuring cup to spoon flour into the ½-cup measuring cup, flatten off the top, and pour the flour into the mixing bowl. Stir well with a silicone spatula until blended and you can't see any more flour. (If the batter looks gritty, you're on the right track!)

3. **Bake the brownies.** Pour the batter into your lined pan. Use the spatula to spread evenly. 🛑 Bake for 20–25 minutes (see Make it Your Own tip), or until the top looks cracked with crispy edges.

4. **Let the brownies cool and slice them.** Allow the brownies to cool before removing from the pan, about 1 hour. Place them on a cutting board and cut into 9 squares with a kid-safe knife.

MAKE IT YOUR OWN

For fudgy results, bake for 20 minutes. Want a more cake-like texture? Bake for 25 minutes.

I MADE IT MY OWN BY:

....

....

....

....

....

? DID YOU KNOW?

Hazelnuts grow on trees. June 1 is National Hazelnut Cake Day!

Dirt Cups with
Candy Worms *page 50*

3

cakes & cupcakes

It doesn't have to be a birthday to celebrate with these sweet treats! From a colorful rainbow pound cake to gooey chocolate lava and a strawberry ice cream cone that's baked in the oven, these delicious desserts will be the hit of any special day.

hot fudge lava cakes

Don't let the ordinary look of these cakes fool you—cut them open and you'll find a river of gooey, sweet chocolate!

PREP TIME
20 minutes

COOK TIME
10 minutes

MAKES
8
INDIVIDUAL CAKES

NUT-FREE VEGETARIAN

KITCHEN TOOLS YOU WILL NEED

Paper towel

Muffin pan

Microwave-safe bowl

Medium bowl

Measuring cups

Measuring spoons

Whisk

Silicone spatula or wooden mixing spoon

Ice cream scoop

Cutting board

 **Softened:**
Take your butter out of the refrigerator 30 minutes before you start baking to make sure it is soft.

INGREDIENTS YOU WILL NEED

1 tablespoon **butter**, softened * for greasing the pan, plus ½ cup (1 stick), melted

½ cup **semisweet chocolate chips**

2 whole **eggs**

3 **egg yolks**

1¼ cups **powdered sugar**

1 teaspoon **vanilla extract**

½ cup **all-purpose flour**

I MADE THIS
RECIPE ON:
(DATE)

- - - - - - - - - - - - - - - - - - - -

IT TASTED:
(CIRCLE
THE STARS)

★ ★ ★ ★ ★

WHO
HELPED?

- - - - - - - - - - - - - - - - - - - -

- - - - - - - - - - - - - - - - - - - -

- - - - - - - - - - - - - - - - - - - -

JUST FOR
LAUGHS

**What did one volcano
say to the other?**

I Lava you.

DIRECTIONS

1. Preheat the oven and prepare the pan. 🛑 Preheat the oven to 425°F. Use a paper towel to spread 1 tablespoon of butter inside 8 cups of a muffin pan.

2. Melt the butter and chocolate chips. In a large microwave-safe bowl, melt the ½ cup of butter and chocolate chips. Cook in the microwave for 30 seconds at a time, stirring in between until liquefied (about 60 seconds total).

3. Prepare the eggs. Crack 1 egg into a medium bowl and remove any shell. Repeat with the second egg. For the 3 egg yolks, separate the eggs easily by cracking 1 egg at a time over the sink. Pour the egg into a clean palm and allow the whites to slip through your fingers. Place the yolks in the mixing bowl. Stir to combine.

4. Mix the batter.
Whisk together the sugar and melted chocolate, making sure that there are no lumps. Add the egg mixture, vanilla, and flour. To add the flour correctly, use a second measuring cup to spoon flour into the ½-cup measuring cup, flatten off the top, and pour the flour into the mixing bowl. Stir gently until completely mixed, scraping down the sides of the bowl with a silicone spatula or wooden mixing spoon as needed.

5. Bake the cakes. Use an ice cream scoop to spoon the batter evenly into the 8 buttered muffin cups. 🛑 Bake for 8 minutes (extra gooey inside) to 10 minutes (slightly runny inside).

6. Serve the cakes. Allow the cakes to cool for 3 to 5 minutes. 🛑 Place a cutting board on top of the muffin pan, then flip the pan so the cakes gently fall. Carefully serve the cakes on small plates and top with ice cream or whipped cream.

❓ DID YOU KNOW?

Only the edges of these cakes are fully cooked. That's why the center stays runny!

lemon cake with raspberry sauce 🧤🧤

Got a grown-up you want to impress? This is the perfect cake to bake for any special day. It's not too sweet but it is oh-so-tender with every bite.

PREP TIME
10 minutes

COOK TIME
45 minutes

MAKES
10 TO 12
SERVINGS

NUT-FREE
VEGETARIAN

KITCHEN TOOLS YOU WILL NEED

Paper towel

Bundt pan

Measuring spoons

Zester

Cutting board

Kid-safe knife

Stand mixer or large mixing bowl with electric beaters

Measuring cups

Medium mixing bowl

Silicone spatula or wooden mixing spoon

Toothpick

Fork

Pastry brush or spoon

Piping bag or plastic baggie (optional)

INGREDIENTS YOU WILL NEED

For the cake

1 tablespoon **butter**, softened for greasing the pan

2 tablespoons **all-purpose flour**, plus 2½ cups

4 **lemons**, zested

2 **lemons**, juiced

1½ cups **granulated sugar**

3 teaspoons **baking powder**

½ teaspoon **salt**

¾ cup **buttermilk**

¾ cup **canola oil**

4 **eggs**

For the glaze

2 **lemons**, juiced

1 cup **powdered sugar**

½ cup **raspberry jam**

Softened:
Take your butter out of the refrigerator 30 minutes before you start baking to make sure it is soft.

DIRECTIONS

1. Preheat the oven and prepare the pan. 🛑 Preheat the oven to 325°F. Use a paper towel to spread the butter on the inside of a Bundt pan. Sprinkle 2 tablespoons of flour into the pan and shake back and forth until flour covers the inside of the pan. The butter and flour combination will keep the cake from sticking to the pan. Shake any extra flour into the garbage can.

2. Mix the batter. Use a zester to scrape the yellow part of the lemon peels onto a plate. Using a cutting board and kid-safe knife, cut 2 of the lemons in half and squeeze the juice into a stand mixer or large mixing bowl. Remove any seeds. Add the lemon zest to the bowl plus the sugar, baking powder, salt, buttermilk, and oil. In a medium bowl, crack 1 egg. Remove any shell and pour the egg into the large bowl. Repeat with the remaining eggs.

3. Add the flour and mix. To add the flour correctly, use a second measuring cup to spoon flour into the 1-cup measuring cup, flatten off the top, pour the flour into the mixing bowl, and repeat. Repeat once more with the ½-cup measuring cup. Beat for 3 minutes at medium speed.

4. Bake the cake. Pour the batter into the prepared Bundt pan. 🛑 Bake for 40 to 45 minutes, until a toothpick inserted into the middle of the cake comes out clean.

5. Make the glaze. Using a cutting board and kid-safe knife, slice the remaining 2 lemons. Squeeze the juice into a medium mixing bowl, fishing out any seeds. Add powdered sugar. Stir carefully until the glaze is smooth (makes about ½ cup).

6. Add the glaze to the cake. 🛑 Remove the cake from the oven. With the hot cake still in the pan, use a fork to prick every inch of the bottom of the cake. Use a pastry brush or spoon to drizzle half of the glaze over the hot cake in the pan. Let stand for 10 minutes. 🛑 Place a serving plate on top of the cake and flip the pan. With the cake resting on the plate, brush or spoon the remaining glaze over the top.

7. Prepare the raspberry sauce. 🛑 Spoon the raspberry jam into a piping bag or plastic baggie, then cut the very tip of the bag off. Squeeze the bag in a zig-zag pattern over the top of the cake. Or just serve a dollop of jam on the side of every slice.

RECIPE TIP

If you don't have buttermilk, you can add a teaspoon of lemon juice or vinegar to regular milk and let it sit for 3 to 5 minutes.

DID YOU KNOW?

A lemon tree can survive more than 100 years.

strawberry ice cream cone cupcakes

No need to freeze these ice cream cones—you'll find sweet strawberry cake baked right inside, topped with a scoop of fresh strawberry icing.

PREP TIME
20 minutes

COOK TIME
20 minutes

MAKES
24
CUPCAKES

NUT-FREE
VEGETARIAN

KITCHEN TOOLS YOU WILL NEED

Stand mixer or large mixing bowl with electric beaters

Measuring cups

Medium bowl

Silicone spatula or wooden mixing spoon

Measuring spoons

Sifter

Kid-safe knife

2 muffin pans

Toothpick

Piping bag, plastic baggie, or ice cream scoop

INGREDIENTS YOU WILL NEED

For the cake

½ cup **butter** (1 stick), **softened**﹡

1 cup **granulated sugar**

2 **eggs**

⅓ cup **strawberry jam** or **fruit spread**

¼ cup **buttermilk**

1 teaspoon **vanilla extract**

1 tablespoon **cornstarch**, plus 1 teaspoon

1⅔ cups **all-purpose flour**

½ teaspoon **baking soda**

½ teaspoon **baking powder**

¼ teaspoon **salt**

3 drops **red food coloring** (optional)

5 to 7 large **strawberries** (about ¾ cup once diced)

24 old-fashioned **ice cream cones**

For the frosting

½ cup **strawberry jam** or **fruit spread**

½ cup **butter** (1 stick), **softened**﹡

8 ounces **cream cheese** (1 brick), **softened**﹡

3 cups **powdered sugar**

½ teaspoon **vanilla extract**

3 drops **red food coloring** (optional)

Softened:
Take your butter and cream cheese out of the refrigerator 30 minutes before you start baking to make sure it is soft.

I MADE THIS
RECIPE ON:
(DATE)

- - - - - - - - - - - - - - - -

IT TASTED:
(CIRCLE
THE STARS)

★ ★ ★ ★ ★

WHO
HELPED?

- - - - - - - - - - - - - - - -

- - - - - - - - - - - - - - - -

- - - - - - - - - - - - - - - -

DIRECTIONS

1. Cream* the sugar. In a stand mixer or large mixing bowl beat the butter and sugar until light and fluffy, about 3 minutes.

2. Add the wet ingredients. In a medium bowl, crack 1 egg. Remove any shell and pour the egg into the large bowl. Mix for 30 seconds. Repeat with the second egg. Use a silicone spatula or wooden mixing spoon to scrape down the sides of the bowl. Add the strawberry jam, buttermilk, and vanilla. Beat until combined, about 30 seconds.

3. Add the dry ingredients. Place a sifter over the mixing bowl and add the cornstarch, flour, baking soda, baking powder, and salt. To add the flour correctly, use a second measuring cup to spoon flour into the 1-cup measuring cup, flatten off the top, and pour the flour into the sifter. Repeat with the ⅔-cup measuring cup. Shake the sifter gently until all the dry ingredients have fallen through to the bowl. Mix on low for about 10 seconds until just combined, adding in the food coloring (if using) as the batter comes together.

4. Add the strawberries. Use a kid-safe knife to cut the strawberries into pieces about as big as a pencil eraser. Pour the cut strawberries into the batter and mix gently with the spatula.

5. Bake the cupcakes. 🛑 Preheat the oven to 350°F. Place the ice cream cones right-side-up in 2 muffin pans. Fill each cone ONLY three-quarters full. Do not overfill, or the cupcakes will overflow. 🛑 Bake for 15 to 18 minutes, until a toothpick inserted into the middle of a cupcake comes out clean.

6. Prepare the frosting. Combine the jam, butter, cream cheese, powdered sugar, vanilla, and food coloring (if using). Beat on medium speed until fluffy, about 2 minutes. Refrigerate while the cupcakes cool.

7. Frost the cupcakes. Allow the cupcakes to cool completely before frosting. Use a piping bag, plastic baggie with the tip cut off, or ice cream scoop to top each cupcake with lots of frosting.

Cream: Whip butter together with sugar until fluffy.

MAKE IT YOUR OWN

To make these cupcakes extra special, add whipped cream, sprinkles, and a strawberry on top!

I MADE IT MY OWN BY:

....

....

....

....

....

RECIPE TIP

If you don't have buttermilk, you can add a teaspoon of lemon juice or vinegar to regular milk and let it sit for 3 to 5 minutes.

rainbow surprise pound cake 🧤🧤🧤

This might look like your average loaf cake but wait until you cut it open! A rainbow surprise waits inside.

PREP TIME
20 minutes

COOK TIME
55 minutes

MAKES
8
SERVINGS

NUT-FREE
VEGETARIAN

KITCHEN TOOLS YOU WILL NEED

Paper towel

8½-by-4½-inch or 9-by-5-inch loaf pan

Measuring cups

Stand mixer or large mixing bowl with electric beaters

3 medium bowls

Silicone spatula

Measuring spoons

4 spoons

Toothpick

Microwave-safe bowl

Whisk

✱ Softened: Take your butter out of the refrigerator–tor 30 minutes before you start baking to make sure it is soft.

INGREDIENTS YOU WILL NEED

For the cake

1 tablespoon **butter**, for greasing the pan, plus 1 cup (2 sticks), softened ✱

1 tablespoon **all-purpose flour**, plus 2 cups

1 cup **granulated sugar**

4 **eggs**

2 teaspoons **vanilla extract**

Food coloring (blue, red, green, and yellow)

For the glaze

3 tablespoons **butter**, melted

1 cup **powdered sugar**

2 teaspoons **vanilla extract**

2 tablespoons **milk**

Sprinkles (about 2 tablespoons, optional)

I MADE THIS
RECIPE ON:
(DATE)

IT TASTED:
(CIRCLE
THE STARS)

WHO
HELPED?

- - - - - - - - - - - - - - - -

- - - - - - - - - - - - - - - -

- - - - - - - - - - - - - - - -

JUST FOR
LAUGHS

What bow can't be tied?

A rainbow!

DIRECTIONS

1. Preheat the oven and prepare the pan. 🛑 Preheat the oven to 350°F. Use a paper towel to spread 1 tablespoon of butter inside a loaf pan. Sprinkle 1 tablespoon of flour into the pan, then shake from side to side until flour covers all sides of the pan.

2. Cream * **the sugar.** Use a stand mixer or large mixing bowl with electric beaters to beat the butter and sugar together until fluffy, about 2 minutes.

3. Add the wet ingredients. In a medium bowl, crack 1 egg. Remove any shell and pour the egg into the large bowl. Beat for 30 seconds. Repeat with the remaining eggs. Use a silicone spatula to scrape down the sides of the bowl. Add the vanilla and mix.

* Cream: Whip butter together with sugar until fluffy.

4. Add the dry ingredients. Use another measuring cup to scoop flour into your 1-cup measuring cup and scrape off the top. With the mixer on low, slowly add the flour until just combined. Repeat for the second cup of flour. The batter will be thick.

5. Color the batter. Separate the batter into four parts, using the three bowls plus the original mixing bowl. Add a few drops of food coloring to each and stir until blended: blue, red, green, and yellow.

6. Bake the cake. Use a spoon to place a scoop of batter from each bowl in the prepared pan. Alternate each color until all the batter is in the pan. 🛑 Bake for about 55 minutes, until a toothpick inserted into the middle of the cake comes out clean. Let the cake cool in the pan for 15 minutes. 🛑 Place a serving plate on top of the cake and flip the pan.

7. Prepare the glaze. While the cake cools, melt the butter in a microwave-safe bowl, about 20 seconds. Add the sugar and vanilla to the bowl. **Whisk** ✳ until the glaze is smooth, adding milk as needed to make it thinner and more pourable.

8. Pour the glaze over the cake. Drizzle the glaze over the top of the cake until it's covered with a thick coating of glaze, allowing the glaze to drip down the sides. Top with sprinkles (if using). Serve immediately or wait for the glaze to dry.

MAKE IT YOUR OWN

Try an ombré style, using only one color in several shades: light pink, medium pink, dark pink, and so on. To achieve this look, increase the amount of food coloring in each of the four parts of the batter.

I MADE IT MY OWN BY:

....

....

....

....

....

....

✳ **Whisk:** Use a whisk or fork to stir ingredients.

dirt cups with candy worms

They might look creepy but don't worry. Everyone loves the rich chocolate flavor with a hidden surprise inside.

PREP TIME
20 minutes

COOK TIME
20 minutes

MAKES
24
CUPCAKES

NUT-FREE
VEGETARIAN

KITCHEN TOOLS YOU WILL NEED

2 muffin pans

Cupcake liners

Stand mixer or large mixing bowl with electric beaters

Measuring cups

Measuring spoons

Silicone spatula or wooden mixing spoon

Sifter

Toothpick

Medium mixing bowl

Plastic bag

Rolling pin

INGREDIENTS YOU WILL NEED

For the cake

24 **chocolate sandwich cookies**

2 **eggs**

½ cup **granulated sugar**

½ cup packed **brown sugar**

⅓ cup **canola oil**

2 teaspoons **vanilla extract**

½ cup **buttermilk**

¾ cup **all-purpose flour**

½ cup **unsweetened cocoa powder**

1 teaspoon **baking powder**

½ teaspoon **baking soda**

½ teaspoon **salt**

For the frosting

½ cup **butter**, (1 stick) softened

8 ounces **cream cheese**, (1 stick) softened

3 cups **powdered sugar**

1 teaspoon **vanilla extract**

6 **chocolate sandwich cookies**, filling removed and crushed

12 **candy worms**

Softened:
Take your butter and cream cheese out of the refrigerator 30 minutes before you start baking to make sure it is soft.

DIRECTIONS

1. Preheat the oven and prepare the pan. 🛑 Preheat the oven to 350°F. Line 2 muffin pans with cupcake liners. Add 1 chocolate sandwich cookie to the bottom of each cup.

2. Mix the wet ingredients. In a stand mixer or large mixing bowl, crack 1 egg. Remove any shell and repeat with the second egg. Add the granulated sugar, brown sugar, oil, vanilla, and buttermilk. Beat with the mixer or electric beaters for 30 seconds. Use a silicone spatula or wooden mixing spoon to scrape down the sides of the bowl.

3. Add the dry ingredients. Place a sifter over the mixing bowl. To measure the flour correctly, use a second measuring cup to spoon flour into the ¾-cup measuring cup and flatten off the top. Add the flour, cocoa powder, baking powder, baking soda, and salt to the sifter and shake gently until all the dry ingredients have fallen through to the bowl. Mix on low for about 20 seconds, until just combined.

4. Bake the cupcakes. Fill each cupcake liner ONLY half full. Do not overfill or the cupcakes will overflow. 🛑 Bake for 10 to 13 minutes, until a toothpick inserted into the middle of a cupcake comes out clean.

5. Prepare the frosting. In a medium mixing bowl, combine the butter, cream cheese, sugar, and vanilla. Whip on high speed for 1 minute until light and fluffy.

6. Frost the cupcakes. Allow the cupcakes to cool completely before frosting. Scrape the white frosting off the inside of the 6 chocolate sandwich cookies. Place the black cookies into a plastic bag and use a rolling pin to smash them into tiny pieces. Top each cupcake with a generous amount of frosting. Sprinkle with chocolate sandwich pieces and place a candy worm on top.

RECIPE TIP

If you don't have buttermilk, you can add a teaspoon of lemon juice or vinegar to regular milk and let it sit for 3 to 5 minutes.

? DID YOU KNOW?

Chocolate melts in your mouth because it's the only food that liquefies at 93°F. That's colder than the average human body temperature.

Triple
Apple-Cinnamon
Muffins with
Whole Wheat Flour
page 64

muffins

From zucchini muffins studded with sweet cranberries to apple-cinnamon muffins so light they melt in your mouth, there's nothing better than a freshly baked muffin!

zippy zucchini-cranberry muffins 🧤🧤

Who knew a muffin full of veggies could be so yummy? Dazzle your family with a batch of my kids' favorite muffins.

PREP TIME
20 minutes

COOK TIME
20 minutes

MAKES
12
MUFFINS

NUT-FREE
VEGETARIAN

KITCHEN TOOLS YOU WILL NEED

Paper towel

Muffin pan

Grater

Cutting board or plate

Medium bowl

Stand mixer or large mixing bowl

Whisk

Measuring cups

Measuring spoons

Sifter

Silicone spatula

Ice cream scoop

Toothpick

Cooling rack

INGREDIENTS YOU WILL NEED

1 tablespoon **butter** or **nonstick cooking spray**, for greasing the pan

1 cup shredded **zucchini** (about 1 medium zucchini)

2 **eggs**

½ cup **applesauce**

½ cup **plain yogurt**

1 teaspoon **vanilla extract**

2 cups **whole wheat flour**

1 cup **sugar**

1 teaspoon **baking powder**

1 teaspoon **salt**

1 teaspoon **baking soda**

1 teaspoon ground **cinnamon**

1 cup dried **cranberries**

I MADE THIS
RECIPE ON:
(DATE)

- - - - - - - - - - - - - - - - - - - -

IT TASTED:
(CIRCLE
THE STARS)

★ ★ ★ ★ ★

WHO
HELPED?

- - - - - - - - - - - - - - - - - - - -

- - - - - - - - - - - - - - - - - - - -

- - - - - - - - - - - - - - - - - - - -

- - - - - - - - - - - - - - - - - - - -

JUST FOR
LAUGHS

Two muffins are
baking in an oven.
One of them yells,
"Wow, it's hot in
here!" The other
muffin replies:
"Holy cow! A talking
muffin!"

DIRECTIONS

1. Preheat the oven and prepare the pan. 🛑
Preheat the oven to 375°F. Use a paper towel to
spread the butter over the inside of each cup in
the muffin pan, or coat each cup with nonstick
cooking spray.

2. Rinse and grate the zucchini. Wash the
zucchini. 🛑 Use a grater to shred the zucchini
onto a cutting board or plate. Don't cut the ends
off the zucchini. Hold on to the hard end like a
handle and grate until you run out of zucchini.

**3. Mix the wet
ingredients.** In a
medium bowl, crack
1 egg. Remove any shell
and pour the egg into
the bowl of a stand
mixer or a large mixing
bowl. Repeat with the
second egg and whisk
until frothy. Add the
applesauce, yogurt, and
vanilla. Whisk again.

4. Add the dry ingredients to the wet ingredients. Place a sifter over the bowl with the wet ingredients and add the flour, sugar, baking powder, salt, baking soda, and cinnamon. To add the flour correctly, use a second measuring cup to spoon flour into the 1-cup measuring cup, flatten off the top, pour the flour into the sifter, and repeat. Shake the sifter carefully until all the dry ingredients have fallen through to the mixing bowl. Using a silicone spatula, gently stir the mixture 3 to 5 times until you don't see any more flour in the batter.

5. Add the zucchini and dried cranberries. Finish by adding the shredded zucchini and dried cranberries. Stir until just combined.

6. Bake the muffins. Using an ice cream scoop to measure the batter, fill each cup of the muffin pan about three-quarters full. (STOP) Bake in the oven for 20 minutes, or until a toothpick inserted into the middle of a muffin comes out clean. The muffins should be puffy and slightly browned.

7. Cool and serve. Allow the baked muffins to cool for 10 minutes, then remove each muffin from the pan and place on a cooling rack—or enjoy right away! If you have leftover muffins, store them, covered, at room temperature for up to 2 days or in the refrigerator for up to 4 days. Freeze leftover muffins for up to 3 months.

? DID YOU KNOW?

Zucchini is an Italian word meaning many zucchini. One zucchini is really a *zucchina*.

magical muffin pan blueberry scones 🧤

Scones have always been on the menu for teatime, but now they make a delicious meal anytime, anywhere!

PREP TIME
15 minutes
COOK TIME
15 minutes

MAKES
12
SMALL
SCONES

NUT-FREE
VEGETARIAN

KITCHEN TOOLS YOU WILL NEED

Paper towel

Muffin pan

Stand mixer or large mixing bowl with electric beaters

Measuring cups

Measuring spoons

Medium bowl

Silicone spatula

Ice cream scoop

Cooling rack

✳ Softened:
Take your butter out of the refrigerator 30 minutes before you start baking to make sure it is soft.

INGREDIENTS YOU WILL NEED

1 tablespoon **butter**, softened✳ or **nonstick cooking spray**, for greasing the pan, plus ½ cup butter (1 stick), cold and cubed

1½ cups **all-purpose flour**

1¼ cups **old-fashioned oats**

1 tablespoon **baking powder**

½ teaspoon **kosher salt**

¼ cup **granulated sugar**

1 large **egg**

½ cup **buttermilk**

1 teaspoon **apple cider vinegar**

1 teaspoon **vanilla extract**

1 cup fresh or frozen **blueberries**

2 tablespoons **raw sugar** (optional)

I MADE THIS
RECIPE ON:
(DATE)

....

IT TASTED:
(CIRCLE
THE STARS)

★ ★ ★ ★ ★

WHO
HELPED?

....

....

....

JUST FOR
LAUGHS

What happens to a scone when you have eaten it?

It's scone (s'gone)!

DIRECTIONS

1. Preheat the oven and prepare the pan. 🛑 Preheat the oven to 425°F. Use a paper towel to spread the softened butter over the inside of each cup in the muffin pan, or coat each cup with nonstick cooking spray.

2. Mix the dry ingredients. In a stand mixer or large mixing bowl with electric beaters, blend the flour, oats, baking powder, salt, and sugar on low speed until well mixed, about 30 seconds. To add the flour correctly, use a second measuring cup to spoon flour into the 1-cup measuring cup, flatten off the top, and pour the flour into the mixing bowl. Repeat with the ½-cup measuring cup.

3. Add the butter. Add the cubed cold butter and mix again until you see uniform chunks of batter, about 2 minutes.

4. Add the wet ingredients. In a medium bowl, crack the egg. Remove any shell and pour the egg into the large mixing bowl or the bowl of the stand mixer. Add the buttermilk, vinegar, and vanilla. Beat again until just mixed, about 30 seconds.

5. Pour in the blueberries. Add the blueberries. Use the silicone spatula to gently fold※ the blueberries into the dough.

6. Bake. Use an ice cream scoop to measure the batter and place it in the muffin pan cups. Use clean hands to flatten the batter in each cup. Sprinkle with the raw sugar (if using). (STOP) Bake for 15 to 17 minutes, until just golden on the outside.

7. Cool. Allow the baked muffins to cool for 10 minutes, then remove each muffin from the pan and place on a cooling rack—or enjoy right away!

> ※ **Fold:** Stir gently with a spatula using a folding motion, so the ingredients don't break apart.

RECIPE TIP

If you don't have buttermilk, you can add a teaspoon of lemon juice or vinegar to regular milk and let it sit for 3 to 5 minutes.

? DID YOU KNOW?

The first scones are believed to have been baked in Scotland.

triple apple-cinnamon muffins with whole wheat flour 🧤🧤

How many ways can you get an apple into a muffin? In this recipe, you'll use applesauce, grated apples, and chopped apples, too!

PREP TIME
25 minutes

COOK TIME
20 minutes

MAKES
12
MUFFINS

NUT-FREE
VEGETARIAN

KITCHEN TOOLS YOU WILL NEED

Paper towel

Muffin pan

Apple slicer

Cutting board

Kid-safe knife

Grater

Stand mixer or large mixing bowl with electric beaters

Measuring cups

Measuring spoons

Medium bowl

Sifter

Silicone spatula

Ice cream scoop

Toothpick

Cooling rack

INGREDIENTS YOU WILL NEED

1 tablespoon **butter**, softened* or **nonstick baking spray**, for greasing the pan, plus ½ cup butter (1 stick), melted

2 **apples**

1 cup **sugar**

2 **eggs**

½ cup plain **Greek yogurt**

½ cup **applesauce**

1 teaspoon **vanilla extract**

1¾ cups **whole wheat flour**

1½ teaspoons **baking powder**

1 teaspoon ground **cinnamon**

½ teaspoon **baking soda**

½ teaspoon **salt**

1 tablespoon **raw sugar** (optional)

Softened:
Take your butter out of the refrigerator 30 minutes before you start baking to make sure it is soft.

I MADE THIS
RECIPE ON:
(DATE)

- - - - - - - - - - - - - - - - - - - -

IT TASTED:
(CIRCLE
THE STARS)

★ ★ ★ ★ ★

WHO
HELPED?

- - - - - - - - - - - - - - - - - - - -

- - - - - - - - - - - - - - - - - - - -

- - - - - - - - - - - - - - - - - - - -

JUST FOR
LAUGHS

Who lives in an apple and likes to read?

A bookworm!

DIRECTIONS

1. Preheat the oven and prepare the pan. 🛑 Preheat the oven to 425°F. Use a paper towel to spread the butter over the inside of each cup in the muffin pan, or coat each cup with nonstick cooking spray.

2. Rinse and prepare the apples. Rinse the apples. 🛑 Core the apple with an apple slicer. Using a cutting board and a kid-safe knife, chop 1 apple into ½-inch pieces, about as big as a dime. 🛑 Grate a second apple over the cutting board.

3. Mix the wet ingredients. In a stand mixer or a large mixing bowl with electric beaters, add the butter and sugar, beating together until combined. In a medium bowl, crack 1 egg. Remove any shell and pour the egg into the large bowl. Repeat with the second egg. Beat well with the mixer or electric beaters. Add the yogurt, applesauce, and vanilla and beat again.

4. Sift ＊ **in the dry ingredients.** Place a sifter over the mixing bowl and add the flour, baking powder, cinnamon, baking soda, and salt. Shake the sifter gently until all the dry ingredients have fallen through to the bowl.

5. Add the apples to the batter. Add the grated and chopped apples then use the silicone spatula to stir to combine.

＊ **Sift:** Shake dry ingredients through a mesh sifter to remove any lumps.

6. Bake the muffins. Divide the batter evenly between the 12 muffin cups using an ice cream scoop. Sprinkle the tops of the muffins with raw sugar (if using). 🛑 Bake the muffins for 17 to 18 minutes, or until the muffins are golden on top and a toothpick inserted into the middle of a muffin comes out clean.

7. Cool. Allow the baked muffins to cool for 10 minutes, then remove each muffin from the pan and place on a cooling rack—or enjoy right away!

sweet potato–walnut muffins

This recipe combines the rich flavor of sweet potatoes with protein-packed walnuts for a one-bowl recipe you'll want to make over and over again.

PREP TIME
20 minutes

COOK TIME
20 minutes

MAKES
12
MUFFINS

VEGETARIAN

KITCHEN TOOLS YOU WILL NEED

Paper towel

Muffin pan

Vegetable peeler

Cutting board

Large sharp knife

Food processor

Medium bowl

Measuring spoons

Measuring cups

Ice cream scoop

Toothpick

Cooling rack

INGREDIENTS YOU WILL NEED

1 tablespoon **butter** or **nonstick baking spray**, for greasing the pan

1 large **sweet potato**, peeled and cut into large chunks

1¼ cups **walnuts**

2 **eggs**

½ cup **olive oil**

2 teaspoons **vanilla extract**

1 cup **granulated sugar**

2 teaspoons **baking powder**

2 teaspoons ground **cinnamon**

½ teaspoon **salt**

1¾ cups **whole wheat flour**

I MADE THIS
RECIPE ON:
(DATE)

IT TASTED:
(CIRCLE
THE STARS)

★ ★ ★ ★ ★

WHO
HELPED?

JUST FOR
LAUGHS

**Why are sweet
potatoes so busy?**

Because they
don't want to be
couch potatoes!

DIRECTIONS

1. Preheat the oven and prepare the pan. (STOP)
Preheat the oven to 375°F. Use a paper towel to
spread the butter over the inside of each cup in
the muffin pan, or coat each cup with nonstick
cooking spray.

**2. Rinse, peel, and
chop the sweet potato.**
(STOP) Rinse the sweet
potato and peel it with
a vegetable peeler.
(STOP) Then, using a cut-
ting board and a large
sharp knife, cut the
sweet potato into large
chunks, about 8 pieces.

3. Pulse* the nuts.
(STOP) In a food processor, pulse the walnuts until
they're finely ground, about 5 to 6 times.

4. Pulse the sweet potatoes. Add the sweet
potato chunks to the food processor. (STOP) Keep
pulsing until everything is blended together,
about 5 or 6 times.

5. Combine the eggs. In a medium bowl, crack
1 egg. Remove any shell and pour the egg into
the food processor. Repeat with the second
egg. (STOP) Pulse 2 or 3 times.

6. Add the remaining wet ingredients. Pour the olive oil and vanilla into the food processor. (STOP) Pulse again.

7. Add the remaining dry ingredients. Add the sugar, baking powder, cinnamon, salt, and flour to the food processor. To add the flour correctly, use a second measuring cup to spoon flour into the 1-cup measuring cup, flatten off the top, and pour the flour into the food processor. Repeat with the ¾-cup measuring cup. (STOP) Pulse until just combined.

8. Bake the muffins. Using an ice cream scoop, fill the muffin pan cups three-quarters full. (STOP) Bake for 20 to 22 minutes or until a toothpick inserted into the middle of a muffin comes out clean.

9. Cool. Allow the baked muffins to cool for 10 minutes, then remove each muffin from the pan and place on a cooling rack—or enjoy right away!

RECIPE TIP

Use 1¼ cups almond meal in place of the walnuts, and you'll only have to grind the sweet potatoes. If you're using almond meal, grind the sweet potatoes first, then add the almond meal with the eggs in step 5.

? DID YOU KNOW?

President George Washington grew sweet potatoes on his plantation.

Pulse: Press the button on a food processor for only a couple seconds at a time. Lift up and the machine turns off.

razzle-dazzle raspberry–cream cheese muffins 🧤🧤

Sweet summer berries combine with cool cream cheese to make a muffin that tastes like a fancy pastry!

PREP TIME
20 minutes
COOK TIME
30 minutes

MAKES
12
MUFFINS

NUT-FREE
VEGETARIAN

KITCHEN TOOLS YOU WILL NEED

Muffin pan

Cupcake liners

Stand mixer or large mixing bowl with electric beaters

Medium bowl

Measuring spoons

Measuring cups

Sifter

Silicone spatula

Ice cream scoop

Small spoon

Toothpick

✳ **Softened:**
Take your butter and cream cheese out of the refrigerator 30 minutes before you start baking to make sure it is soft.

INGREDIENTS YOU WILL NEED

4 ounces **cream cheese** (½ brick), divided and softened✳

2 tablespoons **butter**, softened✳

½ cup **sugar**

2 **eggs**

3 tablespoons **buttermilk**

½ teaspoon **vanilla extract**

¾ cup **all-purpose flour**

½ teaspoon **baking powder**

½ teaspoon **baking soda**

½ teaspoon **salt**

1 cup **fresh raspberries**

I MADE THIS
RECIPE ON:
(DATE)

....

IT TASTED:
(CIRCLE
THE STARS)

★ ★ ★ ★ ★

WHO
HELPED?

....

....

....

....

JUST FOR
LAUGHS

**What do ghosts put
on their bagels?**

Scream cheese!

DIRECTIONS

1. Preheat the oven and prepare the pan. 🛑
Preheat the oven to 350°F. Line a muffin pan
with paper liners.

2. Cream ❋ **the butter.** In a stand mixer or
large mixing bowl with electric beaters, mix half
of the cream cheese with the butter and sugar
until smooth, about 2 minutes.

3. Add the eggs. In
a medium bowl, crack
1 egg. Remove any shell
and pour the egg into
the large bowl. Repeat
with the second egg.
Beat until creamy, about
1 minute.

**4. Add the wet
ingredients.** Pour in
the buttermilk and
vanilla. Beat again for
30 seconds.

5. Add the dry ingredients. Place a sifter
over the mixing bowl and add the flour, baking
powder, baking soda, and salt. To add the flour
correctly, use a second measuring cup to spoon
flour into the ¾-cup measuring cup, flatten off

the top, and pour the flour into the sifter. Shake the sifter gently until all the dry ingredients have fallen through to the bowl. Gently mix on low for 30 to 40 seconds.

6. **Add the raspberries.** Pour the raspberries into the mixing bowl and gently stir with a silicone spatula.

7. **Fill the muffin pan.** Use an ice cream scoop to measure the batter, filling each cup of your muffin pan three-quarters full.

8. **Top with the cream cheese.** Use a small spoon to make pea-sized scoops of the remaining cream cheese and place 2 or 3 scoops on top of each muffin.

9. **Bake the muffins.** 🛑 Bake for 25 to 28 minutes or until a toothpick inserted into the middle of a muffin comes out clean.

10. **Cool.** Allow the baked muffins to cool for 10 minutes, then remove each muffin from the pan and place on a cooling rack—or enjoy right away!

 **Cream:** Whip butter and cream cheese together with sugar until fluffy.

 RECIPE TIP

Frozen berries will work. Add 2 extra tablespoons of flour to absorb the extra moisture.

If you don't have buttermilk, you can add a teaspoon of lemon juice or vinegar to regular milk and let it sit for 3 to 5 minutes.

? DID YOU KNOW?

The average raspberry has 100 to 200 seeds!

Roly-Poly
Cinnamon-Raisin
Bagels *page 94*

5

pastries

Rich peach cobbler, cinnamon rolls slathered in creamy frosting, chewy bagels, and gooey s'mores pies straight out of the oven. It won't take a trip to a bakery to enjoy any of these sweet treats because you can make them yourself!

easy-peasy peach cobbler

Frozen peaches make this recipe a snap because they're already peeled and sliced.

PREP TIME
20 minutes

COOK TIME
40 minutes

MAKES
6
SERVINGS

EGG-FREE
NUT-FREE
VEGETARIAN

KITCHEN TOOLS YOU WILL NEED

Paper towel

9-by-9-inch [square] or 9-inch [round] baking pan

Microwave-safe bowl

Measuring cups

Measuring spoons

Large mixing bowl

Whisk

Silicone spatula

INGREDIENTS YOU WILL NEED

1 tablespoon **butter** or **nonstick cooking spray**, for greasing the pan, plus ¼ cup butter (½ stick), melted

½ cup **granulated sugar**, plus 1 tablespoon

1 cup **flour**

2 teaspoons **baking powder**

½ teaspoon **salt**

1 teaspoon ground **cinnamon**

½ cup **milk**

2 cups frozen **peaches**, thawed or 4 fresh peaches, sliced

Whipped cream or **vanilla ice cream**, for serving

I MADE THIS
RECIPE ON:
(DATE)

- - - - - - - - - - - - - - - -

IT TASTED:
(CIRCLE
THE STARS)

★ ★ ★ ★ ★

WHO
HELPED?

- - - - - - - - - - - - - - - -

- - - - - - - - - - - - - - - -

- - - - - - - - - - - - - - - -

- - - - - - - - - - - - - - - -

JUST FOR
LAUGHS

Did you hear about
the fruit who made
everyone feel warm
and fuzzy?

She was a real peach.

DIRECTIONS

1. Preheat the oven and prepare the pan. 🛑
Preheat the oven to 350°F. Use a paper towel to
spread 1 tablespoon of butter over the inside
of the baking pan or coat the pan with nonstick
cooking spray.

2. Melt the butter. 🛑 Microwave the ¼ cup
butter in a microwave-safe bowl for 20 seconds.
Repeat if needed.

3. Mix the batter. Combine the melted
butter with ½ cup of sugar, the flour, baking
powder, salt, cinnamon, and milk in a large
mixing bowl. To add the flour correctly, use a
second measuring cup to spoon flour into the
1-cup measuring cup, flatten off the top, and
pour the flour into the mixing bowl. **Whisk**✳
until smooth.

✳ **Whisk: Use a
whisk or fork to
stir ingredients.**

4. **Pour the batter into the pan.** Use a silicone spatula to get every bit of batter out of the bowl and into the baking pan.

5. **Sprinkle with the fruit and sugar.** Add the peaches (but not any extra juice) on top, spreading the slices out evenly. Sprinkle the peaches with the last tablespoon of sugar.

6. **Bake.** (STOP) Place the pan in the oven and bake for 35 to 40 minutes or until the edges of the cobbler are browned.

7. **Serve warm or cold.** Cobbler is delicious with whipped cream or a scoop of vanilla ice cream.

? DID YOU KNOW?

The only difference between a peach and a nectarine is the texture of their skin. (Peaches are fuzzy!)

shortcut cinnamon rolls

Cinnamon rolls fresh from the oven usually take hours. But this supersmart method gives you mouthwatering results in a snap.

PREP TIME
20 minutes

COOK TIME
20 minutes

MAKES
24
ROLLS

NUT-FREE
VEGETARIAN

KITCHEN TOOLS YOU WILL NEED

Paper towel

Muffin pan

Microwave-safe bowl

Stand mixer

Measuring cups

Measuring spoons

Cookie scoop

Small bowl

Medium bowl

Silicone spatula

Ice cream scoop

Toothpick

Cooling rack

INGREDIENTS YOU WILL NEED

For the rolls

1 tablespoon **butter** or **nonstick cooking spray**, for greasing the pan, plus ¼ cup butter (½ stick), melted

3 cups **flour**

½ cup **sugar**

¼ teaspoon **salt**

4 teaspoons **baking powder**

1½ cups **milk**

2 teaspoons **vanilla extract**

2 **eggs**

For the swirl filling

1 cup **butter** (2 sticks), **softened**✳

½ cup **brown sugar**

1 tablespoon ground **cinnamon**

For the glaze

8 ounces **cream cheese** (1 brick), **softened**✳

½ cup **powdered sugar**

1 tablespoon **milk**

✳ **Softened:** Take your butter and cream cheese out of the refrigerator 30 minutes before you start baking to make sure it is soft.

I MADE THIS
RECIPE ON:
(DATE)

IT TASTED:
(CIRCLE
THE STARS)

★ ★ ★ ★ ★

WHO
HELPED?

JUST FOR
LAUGHS

**Why did the
cinnamon roll?**

Because she saw an
apple turn over.

DIRECTIONS

1. Preheat the oven and prepare the pan. (STOP) Preheat the oven to 350°F. Use a paper towel to spread 1 tablespoon of butter over the inside of each cup in the muffin pan.

2. Melt the butter. (STOP) Using a microwave-safe bowl, melt ¼ cup of butter (about 25 seconds in the microwave). Set aside.

3. Prepare the swirl filling. Use the stand mixer to combine the softened butter, brown sugar, and cinnamon. Whip until fluffy. When you see cinnamon everywhere, it's done (about 20 seconds). Turn the mixer off. Use a cookie scoop to measure equally and place 1 scoop on the bottom of each muffin pan cup. Scoop out the rest of the mixture into a small bowl and set aside.

4. Combine the ingredients. Use the stand mixer again (don't worry about any leftover cinnamon mixture) to combine the melted butter, flour, sugar, salt, baking powder, milk, and vanilla. To add the flour correctly, use a second measuring cup to spoon flour into the 1-cup measuring cup, flatten off the top, and pour the flour into the mixing bowl. Repeat two more times. In a medium bowl, crack 1 egg. Remove any shell and pour the egg into the mixer.

Repeat with the second egg. Mix on medium speed until incorporated, about 20 seconds. The batter will have tiny lumps.

5. **Pour the batter into the pan.** Scrape the bottom and sides of the mixing bowl with a silicone spatula and stir in any remaining bits of flour. Use an ice cream scoop to measure batter into the cups of the prepared muffin pan, using the spatula to scrape it out completely.

6. **Top with the cinnamon mixture.** Using a cookie scoop again, drop the cinnamon mixture on top of the cake batter.

7. **Bake.** 🛑 Bake for 20 to 22 minutes or until a toothpick inserted into the center of a "roll" comes out clean. Allow to cool for 5 minutes before touching the pan again.

8. **Prepare the glaze.** While the rolls bake, rinse out the mixer bowl. Add the cream cheese and whip it on high speed until fluffy, about 30 seconds. Stop the mixer and add powdered sugar and milk. Start the mixer on low and beat until smooth, about 30 seconds. Set aside until the rolls are out of the oven and slightly cooled.

9. **Glaze the cinnamon rolls.** 🛑 Flip the pan over onto a cooling rack. When the rolls pop out, drizzle the cream cheese glaze over the bottoms (now the tops). Serve warm or cool.

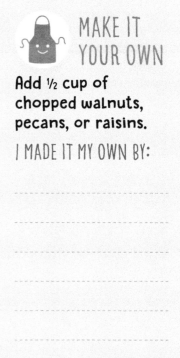

MAKE IT YOUR OWN

Add ½ cup of chopped walnuts, pecans, or raisins.

I MADE IT MY OWN BY:

....

....

....

....

DID YOU KNOW?

Cinnamon comes from the bark of a cinnamon tree, which can grow up to 60 feet tall!

mini s'mores pies 👻👻👻

Gooey, chocolatey and oh-so-delicious, you've never had s'mores—or pie—like this before!

PREP TIME
20 minutes

COOK TIME
25 minutes

MAKES
12
PIES

NUT-FREE
VEGETARIAN

KITCHEN TOOLS YOU WILL NEED

Food processor or plastic bag with a rolling pin

Medium microwave-safe bowl

Measuring cups

Measuring spoons

Muffin pan

Medium bowl

Stand mixer or large mixing bowl with electric beaters

Cutting board

Kid-safe knife

Ice cream scoop

Spoon

INGREDIENTS YOU WILL NEED

For the pie crusts

1½ cups **graham cracker crumbs** (10 full graham crackers ground up)

7 tablespoons **butter** (almost 1 stick), melted

2 tablespoons **sugar**

1 tablespoon **brown sugar**

For the filling

3 **eggs**

4 tablespoons **butter** (½ stick)

8 ounces **semisweet chocolate chips** (1 bag)

7 ounces **marshmallow cream** (1 jar)

1 **chocolate bar**, broken into 12 pieces, for garnish

DIRECTIONS

1. Prepare the graham cracker mixture. Place the graham crackers in a sealed plastic bag and crush with a rolling pin, or 🛑 pulverize them in a food processor. 🛑 Melt the butter in a medium microwave-safe bowl, cooking 20 seconds at a time until liquefied (about 40 seconds total). Combine the crushed graham crackers with the melted butter, then add the sugar and brown sugar and stir.

2. Make the pie crusts. Fill each cup of the muffin pan with the graham cracker mixture. Use a ½-cup measuring cup to press down on the crumbs. Then press the graham crackers up the sides of the muffin pan with clean fingers, until you have what looks like tiny pie crusts.

3. Preheat the oven and beat the eggs. 🛑 Preheat the oven to 325°F. In a medium bowl, crack 1 egg. Remove any shell and pour the egg into the stand mixer or mixing bowl. Repeat with the remaining eggs. Beat until they're yellow and fluffy, about 3 minutes.

4. Prepare the chocolate mixture. Rinse out the graham cracker bowl. Using a cutting board and a kid-safe knife, cut the butter into 4 pieces and place in the bowl along with the chocolate chips. 🛑 Microwave for 10 seconds at a time until melted, about 30 seconds total.

5. Combine the ingredients. Add ½ cup of the chocolate mixture to the eggs and whip again for 20 seconds. Add the rest of the chocolate to the eggs and whip for 20 seconds.

6. Fill the pie crusts with chocolate and marshmallow. Use an ice cream scoop to evenly divide the chocolate batter into each of the pie crusts. Use a buttered spoon or ice cream scoop to scoop a small amount of marshmallow cream on top of each pie.

7. Bake. Bake for 20 to 25 minutes, until the filling is fluffy and slightly browned on top. Garnish with a piece of chocolate bar. Serve warm or chilled. (Note: The tops of the pies will deflate the longer they cool.)

RECIPE TIP

Save a step and buy premade graham cracker crusts at the store! They're bigger, so you'll make six pies that way, but they'll be every bit as good.

summer sweet strawberry tart

This tart is the sweet taste of summer on a fork! Light and flaky crust with a juicy filling, you can use any kind of fruit, fresh or frozen, any time of year.

PREP TIME
40 minutes

COOK TIME
20 minutes

MAKES
6 TO 8
SERVINGS

NUT-FREE
VEGETARIAN

KITCHEN TOOLS YOU WILL NEED

Measuring cups

Measuring spoons

Stand mixer with paddle attachment or large mixing bowl and pastry cutter

Silicone spatula or wooden mixing spoon

Cutting board

Kid-safe knife

Plastic wrap

Rolling pin

Baking sheet

Parchment paper or silicone baking mat

Small bowl

Fork

Pastry brush

INGREDIENTS YOU WILL NEED

2½ cups **all-purpose flour**, plus 2 tablespoons (if you are using frozen fruit)

¼ cup **sugar**, plus 1 tablespoon

1 cup **butter** (2 sticks), cold and cubed

2 teaspoons **vanilla extract**

¼ cup **ice water**

2 cups **strawberries**, sliced

Handful of **flour** for rolling

1 **egg**

I MADE THIS
RECIPE ON:
(DATE)

- - - - - - - - - - - -

IT TASTED:
(CIRCLE
THE STARS)

★ ★ ★ ★ ★

WHO
HELPED?

- - - - - - - - - - - -

- - - - - - - - - - - -

- - - - - - - - - - - -

JUST FOR
LAUGHS

**How do you make a
strawberry shake?**

Put it into the
freezer until
it shivers!

DIRECTIONS

1. **Mix the flour and sugar.** Place the flour and sugar in the stand mixer or large mixing bowl and stir until well mixed. To measure the flour correctly, use a second measuring cup to spoon flour into the 1-cup measuring cup, flatten off the top, pour the flour into the mixing bowl, and repeat. Repeat once more with the ½-cup measuring cup.

2. **Add the butter.** Using a cutting board and a kid-safe knife, slice the sticks of butter into 8 pieces each. Add the butter to the flour mixture and turn on the mixer or use the pastry cutter to blend the butter until you have what looks like white peas.

3. **Add the liquid.** Pour the vanilla into the mixture and stir with the silicone spatula or wooden spoon. Add the ice water 1 tablespoon at a time and stir. When you are able to make a ball with the dough, stop adding water.

4. **Chill the dough.** Use clean hands to make a ball with the dough. Cover the ball in plastic wrap and place in the refrigerator for 20 minutes.

5. **Prepare the berries.** If using fresh strawberries, use a cutting board and a kid-safe knife to slice the tops off and cut each berry in half, lengthwise. If using frozen strawberries, cut the bag open. Add 2 tablespoons of flour to the bag and shake.

6. **Roll the dough.** After 20 minutes, place a handful of flour on a clean counter or cutting board. Use the rolling pin to flatten the dough into a circle 10 to 12 inches wide (about the length of your arm from your elbow to your wrist.)

7. **Assemble the tart.** 🛑 Preheat the oven to 450°F. Line a baking sheet with a piece of parchment paper or a silicone baking mat. 🛑 Roll the dough onto your rolling pin and transfer it to the middle of the baking sheet. Pour the strawberries into the middle. Sprinkle the strawberries with 1 tablespoon of sugar. Fold the edges of the crust up all the way around the tart so 2 inches of the dough rests on top of the berries. It should look like a strawberry pizza with a thick crust.

8. **Brush and bake.** In a small bowl, crack the egg and remove any shell. Use a fork to **whisk** ❉ it until well mixed. Use a pastry brush to coat the part of the crust that's resting on the berries. 🛑 Place the baking sheet in the oven and bake for 20 minutes, until the berries are bubbly and the crust is golden brown.

9. **Cool and serve.** Allow the tart to cool for at least 10 minutes before serving.

RECIPE TIP

Make the dough ahead of time and store it in the refrigerator for up to 3 days. Allow it to warm up on a counter for about 20 minutes before rolling it out.

❉ Whisk: **Use a whisk or fork to stir ingredients.**

roly-poly cinnamon-raisin bagels 🧤🧤🧤

These bagels are chewy on the outside and pillowy soft on the inside. Serve toasted with butter, cream cheese, or just as they are.

PREP TIME
1 hour 15 minutes

COOK TIME
30 minutes

MAKES
8
LARGE BAGELS

NUT-FREE
VEGETARIAN

KITCHEN TOOLS YOU WILL NEED

Stand mixer with dough hook or large mixing bowl

Measuring cups

Measuring spoons

Paper towel

Large bowl

Clean kitchen towel

Large pot

Cutting board

Kid-safe knife

Slotted spoon

Parchment paper or silicone baking mat

Baking sheet

Small bowl

Pastry brush

INGREDIENTS YOU WILL NEED

2¼ teaspoons **active dry yeast** (1 packet)

2 tablespoons **brown sugar**

1½ cups **warm water** (start with ½ cup boiling water, add tap water, alternating until it feels like bath water)

4 cups **bread flour**, plus more for kneading

2 tablespoons ground **cinnamon**, plus 1 teaspoon

1 teaspoon **salt**

½ cup **raisins** (2 snack size boxes, 1 ounce)

Vegetable or **olive oil**, for greasing the proofing bowl

1 **egg**

DIRECTIONS

1. Mix the ingredients. In a stand mixer or large mixing bowl, combine the yeast, brown sugar, warm water, bread flour, cinnamon, salt, and raisins. Stir until the dough starts coming together, about 2 minutes.

2. Knead ❋ the dough. Using a dough hook, knead for 5 minutes on medium speed (you may have to steady the mixer!). Or flip the dough onto a clean counter sprinkled with a handful of flour. Use the heel of your hand to press down, fold the dough in half, and press again over and over for 8 to 10 minutes.

3. Allow the dough to rise. Pour a little oil onto a paper towel and rub the inside of a large bowl until it's well coated. Place the kneaded dough in the bowl. Cover with a clean kitchen towel and set in a warm place (like a sunny window) for 1 hour, until it doubles in size.

4. Boil the water. 🛑 After about 45 minutes, fill a large pot about half full of water and start bringing it to a boil. Turn the heat down and allow it to simmer.

5. Shape the bagels.
When the dough is ready, use a cutting board and a kid-safe knife to slice the dough into 8 wedges, like a pizza. Roll each wedge into a ball. Use your fingers to poke a hole into the center of each one, like a bagel.

6. Cook in hot water. 🛑 Use a slotted spoon to slide the bagels one by one into the boiling water, boiling no more than four at a time. Cook for 2 to 4 minutes, flip and cook for another 2 to 4 minutes. (The longer you boil the bagels, the chewier they'll be.)

7. Prepare to bake. 🛑 Preheat the oven to 425°F. Place each boiled bagel onto a parchment paper–lined baking sheet (or use a silicone baking mat). Crack the egg into a small bowl and remove any shell. Add 1 tablespoon of water and beat together with a fork until the mixture is yellow. Using a pastry brush, brush each bagel with the egg mixture.

8. Bake the bagels. 🛑 Put the baking sheet into the oven and bake for 20 to 25 minutes, until the bagels are golden brown. Remove them from the oven and allow to cool for at least 20 minutes before serving.

MAKE IT YOUR OWN

It's possible to use all-purpose flour, but the results won't be quite as light and chewy.

I MADE IT MY OWN BY:

? DID YOU KNOW?

Bagel comes from a Yiddish word, *beygl*, meaning "ring."

Knead: Use hands to press and fold dough to help it combine and eventually rise.

Take-Along Taco
Hand Pies *page 108*

savory baked goods

From super-cheesy pesto pizza and homemade crackers to tacos you can take to school, these ideas work for anything from lunch to dinner.

french bread pesto pizza

Make your own pesto or buy it from the store, but don't skimp when it comes to slathering it on.

PREP TIME
10 minutes
COOK TIME
10 minutes

MAKES
6
SLICES

EGG-FREE
VEGETARIAN

KITCHEN TOOLS YOU WILL NEED

Food processor

Measuring cups

Measuring spoons

Bread knife

Silicone spatula

Baking sheet

INGREDIENTS YOU WILL NEED

For the pesto

1 cup **fresh basil leaves**

3 **garlic** cloves, peeled

3 tablespoons **pine nuts**

⅓ cup freshly grated **Parmesan cheese**

½ teaspoon **salt**

¼ teaspoon freshly ground **pepper**

⅓ cup **olive oil**

For the pizza

1 long **baguette**

1 cup **fresh mozzarella cheese**, sliced

1 cup **cherry tomatoes**, sliced in half

Fresh basil leaves, for garnish (optional)

JUST FOR
LAUGHS

A customer at a
pizzeria asked:
"Waiter, will my
pizza be long?"

The waiter replied:
"No sir, it'll
be round!"

DIRECTIONS

1. Preheat the oven. 🛑 Preheat the oven to 400°F.

2. Make the pesto. 🛑 In a food processor, combine the basil, garlic, pine nuts, Parmesan cheese, salt, and pepper. Turn the food processor on low and drizzle the olive oil in through the pour spout until combined. Use a clean spoon to taste the pesto and add more salt or pepper as needed.

3. Slice the bread. 🛑 Use a bread knife to slice the baguette in half lengthwise (so it looks like a giant sandwich).

4. **Add the toppings.** Use a silicone spatula to spread a thick layer of pesto on the inside of each piece of bread. Place the bread on the baking sheet, pesto-side up. Lay slices of mozzarella cheese over the top of the pesto.

5. **Bake.** 🛑 Bake in the oven for 8 to 10 minutes, until the mozzarella is melted and bubbly. Top with sliced cherry tomatoes and fresh basil leaves, if you like.

MAKE IT YOUR OWN

Add fresh basil leaves, sliced olives, pepperoni, or sliced mushrooms. Throw a handful of fresh spinach into your pesto mix to boost the flavor—and nutrition!

I MADE IT MY OWN BY:

? DID YOU KNOW?

Pesto comes from the Italian word *pesta* which means "to pound or crush."

no need to knead overnight bread

Wait until you see what a little yeast can do to transform a pile of flour into the tastiest bread you've ever had!

PREP TIME
35 minutes, plus overnight for dough to rest

COOK TIME
50 minutes

MAKES
1
LOAF

EGG-FREE
DAIRY-FREE
NUT-FREE
VEGAN

KITCHEN TOOLS YOU WILL NEED

Large mixing bowl

Measuring cups

Measuring spoons

Silicone spatula

Plastic wrap

Parchment paper

6- to 8-quart covered pot (cast iron, enamel, or ceramic)

INGREDIENTS YOU WILL NEED

3 cups **all-purpose flour**, plus more for dusting

½ teaspoon **instant yeast**

2 teaspoons **salt**

1½ cups **warm water** (about 110°F, like a warm bath)

JUST FOR
LAUGHS

**What did two slices
of bread say to each
other when they saw
a butter dish?**

We're toast.

DIRECTIONS

1. Mix the dough. In a large bowl, mix the flour, yeast, and salt. To add the flour correctly, use a second measuring cup to spoon flour into the 1-cup measuring cup, flatten off the top, and pour the flour into the mixing bowl. Repeat two more times. Add

the warm water and use a silicone spatula to stir until you can't see any more flour. The dough will be sticky and loose.

2. Rest the dough. Cover the bowl with plastic wrap and let it rest at room temperature overnight (at least 12 hours).

3. Place the dough on parchment paper. Put a piece of parchment paper on a clean counter. Sprinkle a handful of flour on top. Flip the bowl over and pour your dough onto the floured parchment paper. Sprinkle another handful of flour on top of the dough. Fold the dough in half two times. Let it rest again, about 30 minutes.

4. Preheat a pot in the oven. (STOP) While the dough rests, preheat the oven to 450°F. Place a large covered pot in the oven. Use potholders to remove the pot after the dough has rested. Using the edges of the parchment paper as handles, place the dough and parchment paper in the pot.

5. Bake. (STOP) Cover the pot with the lid and bake for 40 minutes. Remove the lid and bake for another 10 minutes or until the loaf is golden brown.

MAKE IT YOUR OWN

Add ½ teaspoon of dried rosemary.

I MADE IT MY OWN BY:

? DID YOU KNOW?

The scientific name for active dry yeast is called *Saccharomyces Cerevisiae*, also known as "sugar-eating fungus."

take-along taco hand pies

Use premade pie crust and leftover taco filling—or start from scratch—but don't forget to carve your initial on top.

PREP TIME
45 minutes

COOK TIME
20 minutes

MAKES
4
HAND PIES

NUT-FREE

KITCHEN TOOLS YOU WILL NEED

Large mixing bowl

Measuring spoons

Measuring cups

Silicone spatula

Electric beaters or pastry cutter

Plastic wrap

Skillet

Baking sheet

Parchment paper or silicone baking mat

Rolling pin

Pizza cutter

Fork

Small bowl

Pastry brush

INGREDIENTS YOU WILL NEED

For the pie dough

2½ cups **all-purpose flour**

1 teaspoon **granulated sugar**

½ teaspoon **salt**

1 cup **butter** (2 sticks), chilled

4 tablespoons **ice water**

Handful of **flour**, for rolling

1 **egg**

1 tablespoon **water**

For the filling

1 cup **ground beef or turkey**

1 tablespoon **taco seasoning**

¼ cup **water**

½ cup **cheddar cheese**

I MADE THIS
RECIPE ON:
(DATE)

IT TASTED:
(CIRCLE
THE STARS)

WHO
HELPED?

JUST FOR
LAUGHS

Why can't you trust a taco?

It might spill
the beans!

DIRECTIONS

1. Make the dough. In a large bowl, mix the flour, sugar, and salt with a silicone spatula. Use electric beaters or a pastry cutter to work the butter into the mixture, beating until you have a chunky dough. Gradually add the ice water until you can form a ball.

2. Chill the dough. Wrap the dough in plastic wrap and refrigerate for 20 minutes.

3. Make the taco filling. (STOP) Cook the ground beef or turkey in a skillet, stirring often, on medium heat until browned, about 10 minutes. Add the taco seasoning and water. Simmer for 5 minutes.

4. Preheat the oven and prepare the pan. (STOP) Preheat the oven to 425°F. Line a baking sheet with parchment paper or a silicone baking mat.

5. Roll out the dough. Sprinkle a handful of flour onto a clean surface and use a rolling pin to flatten the dough into a large rectangle, about ¼ inch thick. (STOP) Cut the edges off your dough as needed.

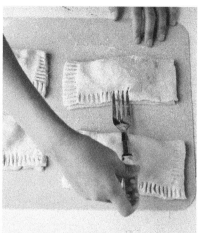

6. **Assemble the taco hand pies.** 🛑 Use a pizza cutter to slice the dough into 4 pieces or kid-safe knife. Place one-quarter of the taco meat on each square and top with the cheddar cheese. Fold one half over the top and use a fork to **crimp** ✳ the edges. Poke your fork into the top of each hand pie to make the shape of an initial.

7. **Brush with egg wash.** 🛑 Place the hand pies on the lined baking sheet. Crack the egg into a small bowl and remove any shell. Add 1 tablespoon of water and **whisk** ✳ with a fork. Use a pastry brush to coat each hand pie with the egg mixture.

8. **Bake.** 🛑 Place the baking sheet in the oven for 15 to 20 minutes, until the edges of the pies are golden brown. *Be careful when biting into a hand pie fresh out of the oven because the filling will be hot!*

MAKE IT YOUR OWN

FiLL your hand pies with cooked ground beef, a dollop of ketchup, and cheese.

I MADE IT MY OWN BY:

....

....

....

? DID YOU KNOW?

Most experts agree that the first tacos were eaten between 1000 and 500 BC!

✳ **Crimp:** Use a fork to squish two layers of dough together to form a seam.

✳ **Whisk:** Use a whisk or fork to stir ingredients.

4-ingredient biscuits

You only need four ingredients to make these biscuits because two of them—the mayonnaise and the self-rising flour—are basically magic.

PREP TIME
5 minutes

COOK TIME
15 minutes

MAKES
12
ROLLS

EGG-FREE
NUT-FREE
VEGETARIAN

KITCHEN TOOLS YOU WILL NEED

Paper towel

Muffin pan

Measuring cups

Measuring spoons

Large mixing bowl

Silicone spatula

Ice cream scoop

Small microwave-safe bowl

Pastry brush

INGREDIENTS YOU WILL NEED

1 tablespoon **butter** or **nonstick cooking spray**, for greasing the pan, plus ¼ cup butter (½ stick)

2 cups **self-rising flour**

1 cup **milk**

¼ cup **mayonnaise**

I MADE THIS
RECIPE ON:
(DATE)

....

IT TASTED:
(CIRCLE
THE STARS)

★ ★ ★ ★ ★

WHO
HELPED?

- - - - - - - - - - - - - - - - -

- - - - - - - - - - - - - - - - -

- - - - - - - - - - - - - - - - -

JUST FOR
LAUGHS

**I don't like
biscuit jokes.**

They're too crumby.

DIRECTIONS

1. Preheat the oven and prepare the pan. (STOP)
Preheat the oven to 375°F. Use a paper towel to
spread butter in every cup of a muffin pan, or
spray with nonstick cooking spray.

2. Mix the ingredients. In the mixing bowl, use
a silicone spatula to stir the flour, milk, and mayonnaise until just mixed together. To measure
the flour correctly, use a second measuring cup
to spoon flour into the 1-cup measuring cup,
flatten off the top, pour the flour into a large
mixing bowl, and repeat.

3. Bake. Use an ice cream scoop to measure the batter into the prepared muffin pan. (STOP) Bake for 12 minutes, until golden brown.

4. Brush with melted butter. (STOP) Microwave the butter in a small bowl for 20 to 30 seconds, until melted. Use a pastry brush to coat each biscuit with butter.

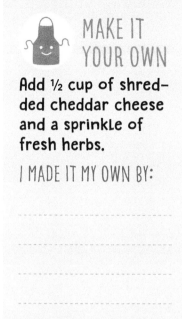

MAKE IT YOUR OWN

Add ½ cup of shredded cheddar cheese and a sprinkle of fresh herbs.

I MADE IT MY OWN BY:

....

....

....

....

....

....

crispy parmesan crackers

Buttery and flaky, these yummy cheese crackers taste better than any fish-shaped snacks you'll ever find at the store.

PREP TIME
20 minutes

COOK TIME
20 minutes

MAKES
4 TO 6
SERVINGS

EGG-FREE
NUT-FREE
VEGETARIAN

KITCHEN TOOLS YOU WILL NEED

Baking sheet

Parchment paper or silicone baking mat

Butter knife

Measuring cups

Measuring spoons

Stand mixer with a paddle attachment or large mixing bowl with electric beaters

Rolling pin

Silicone mat (optional)

Pizza cutter

INGREDIENTS YOU WILL NEED

½ cup **butter** (1 stick)

1 cup **all-purpose flour**

½ teaspoon **salt**

1 cup grated real **Parmesan cheese**

¼ cup **milk**

Handful of **flour**, for rolling

½ teaspoon **coarse salt**, to sprinkle on top

JUST FOR
LAUGHS

**Want to hear
a joke about
Parmesan crackers?**

Never mind, it's
too cheesy.

DIRECTIONS

1. Preheat the oven and prepare the pan. 🛑
Heat the oven to 350°F. Line a baking sheet
with parchment paper or a silicone baking mat.

2. Combine the butter mixture. Use a butter
knife to slice the butter into four pieces. Place
the flour, salt, cheese, and butter into a stand
mixer with a paddle attachment or a large
mixing bowl with electric beaters. To add the
flour correctly, use a second measuring cup
to spoon flour into the 1-cup measuring cup,
flatten off the top, and pour the flour into
the mixing bowl. Mix on medium-low speed
until the flour and butter are combined into a
chunky mixture, about 30 seconds.

3. Add the milk. Pour the milk into the bowl
and mix again until your dough is firm enough
to make a ball.

4. Roll out the dough.
Use a rolling pin to
roll the dough on a sil-
icone mat or a clean
counter with flour sprin-
kled on top. Roll the
dough as thin as you
can, aiming for ¼ inch
(about as thick as a
chopstick).

5. Cut cracker shapes. (STOP) Use a pizza cutter to slice your dough into 1-inch strips one way, then rotate and roll strips the other way. You should have a checkerboard full of squares. Place all the squares on the lined baking sheet except the outer edges.

6. Season with salt. Sprinkle the dough with the coarse salt.

7. Bake. (STOP) Put the baking sheet in the oven for 15 to 20 minutes, rotating it halfway through. Let the crackers cool for 5 minutes and serve.

MAKE IT YOUR OWN

Add dried herbs like rosemary, basil, or oregano.

I MADE IT MY OWN BY:

....

....

....

....

....

DID YOU KNOW?

Parmesan cheese actually tastes better with age.

BAKING WITH KIDS 101
A GUIDE FOR GROWN-UPS

Okay, I'll admit it—you'll rarely find me doing craft projects with my kids. But that's only because I bake with them all the time! Instead of glue, we've got four kinds of flour in our pantry, ready for baking. Every dish we prepare does double duty—it's a memory-maker, but there's a practical upside too: fresh food. The result of our quality time together usually comes in the form of breakfasts, snacks, or desserts.

KITCHEN HACKS

I've been cooking with kids for 10 years now. It hasn't always gone smoothly, but here's what I wish someone would've told me from the beginning: When you're the captain of a tiny cooking team, your job is part motivational speaker and part safety patrol. Here are the best tips I've picked up along the way for keeping everyone happy *and* safe:

- Kids always want to see the inside of the bowl. Set up a sturdy nonslip stool so that they can see every step.
- Even small kids can crack eggs! Here's the trick: Have them break each egg into a little bowl first. Remove any bits of shell, then pour the egg in with the rest of your recipe.
- Worried about vigorous stirring making major messes? Tell kids to start "in slow motion" then work their way up to a faster pace, and use bowls that are bigger than needed. The extra room cuts down on spills.
- Don't be nervous about knives. Show kids how to practice on a banana with a butter knife and move up from there.
- Assign kid-friendly tasks ahead of time. Read through the recipe together and explain which steps can be done by a kid. If there are several kids in the kitchen, divvy the responsibilities up at the start.

- Have a "hands up!" rule. When things get hectic, messy, or on the verge of unsafe (and they will), explain to kids ahead of time that when you say "hands up!" that's exactly what they do—drop what they're holding and put their hands up. It'll give you all a moment to slow down before starting again.
- Prepare for a less than pin-worthy result. Most beginner bakers have a few flops before they master recipes. The goal of baking together at this stage is to have fun, experiment, and taste the results. That's why we've included space to write out how things turned out and what they'd do differently next time.

CHEAT SHEET FOR TEACHING KNIFE, STOVE, AND OVEN SKILLS

The kitchen is a fun place, but there's a reason why kids are often shooed out: It's full of dangerous stuff. But if you banish kids, they'll never learn how to bake—and miss out on a lot of tasty, fun memories. Here's what they need to know:

Real Knives vs. Kid-Safe Knives

Resources for beginner bakers have never been easier to get your hands on. Some of my favorites are nylon knives, crinkle cutters, and safety gloves.

- Nylon knives are usually marketed as "kid-safe" because it's hard to cut yourself with them. They're great for teaching confidence. The downside is that they're serrated. Kids won't learn chopping, only sawing, and the cut is never very precise, so these won't work well for small or delicate items.
- Crinkle cutters are designed to chop fruit and veggies on a cutting board. With a thick handle and wavy blade, kids can easily chop potatoes, cucumbers, and other thick foods. Again, this tool gets the job done but won't teach kids anything about proper knife techniques.

- Safety gloves can be a game changer for kids who want to start using real knives. Their hands will generally be protected while they're learning the basics. If your baker is up for it, a small paring knife is a practical place to start. But beware, even small knives can make big cuts if they're not wearing gloves.

Young kids can start mastering knife skills. These are my top three tips for knife safety:

- **Stand at the right height.** A safe kitchen stool should raise kids to a height where the counter hits their waist and they can easily see and reach everything in front of them.
- **Rock the knife.** Start each cut with the point of the blade and end with the thickest part of the knife on the board. It should feel like they're pushing the knife down and away from themselves.
- **Mind your fingers.** This is the hardest and most important part. Always have a firm grip on whatever you are cutting, but also keep your fingers away from the blade. Curling the tips of your fingers under is a good habit to start with.

Graters and Peelers

For everything from freshly grated cheese to zucchini from the garden, nothing quickly cuts food into tiny shreds better than graters and peelers, but both tools are surprisingly easy to cut yourself with. Here are my best tips for helping kids master them:

- **Graters:** Hold the food in the hand you hold a pencil with and use your other hand to stabilize the grater. Always move in one motion, top to bottom, never up and down. The large holes are perfect for firm foods like cheddar cheese, carrots, and potatoes. The tiny holes work for highly flavorful ingredients you'll typically use less of, like Parmesan cheese or lemon zest. Above all, be aware of your knuckles. Even experienced bakers have grated their share of skin right off.
- **Peelers:** Hold the peeler in the hand you use to write with and steady the food in your other hand. Push the peeler along the skin you want to remove and work in strips, rotating the food each time. Demonstrate first, and consider having small kids use a safety glove to protect their hands.

Using the Stovetop

More than any other tool, the stove seems to be the one that makes parents the most nervous. And I understand why: It's dangerous! But even my second grader uses the stove often, with just a few precautions:

- **Clear everything else off the stove.** The only thing that belongs on a hot stove is a hot pan.
- **Be aware.** This is not the time to daydream or have a dance contest. When you're working with a hot stove, the handle should always be turned in, hair and loose clothes should be pulled back, and kids should be situated on a sturdy stool tall enough so that they can see and reach everything easily.
- **Never leave the pan.** It's just too easy to forget about a hot pan if you step away. I like my kids to stay by the stove's side until this step is over.

Using the Oven

Even though grown-ups typically help with the steps involving an oven, there are a few ways to help kids learn useful skills.

- **Always preheat the oven.** Every recipe in this book will tell you when to start the oven. Don't put it off. Ovens need many minutes to come up to temperature, and since baking involves so much chemistry, the right temperature will be important to get the right results.
- **Be careful with hot pans.** Use thick, dry oven mitts to handle pans coming out of the oven, and always have somewhere to put the pan in mind BEFORE you're holding it in your hands.
- **Watch the door.** When it's time to open the oven door, stand to the side. A big burst of heat often comes streaming out and you don't want to get burned.
- **But don't open the oven door too often.** Instead of letting the hot air escape, use the oven light if you want to take a peek.

MEASUREMENT CONVERSIONS

Volume Equivalents (LIQUID)

US STANDARD	US STANDARD (OUNCES)	METRIC (APPROXIMATE)
2 tablespoons	1 fl. oz.	30 mL
¼ cup	2 fl. oz.	60 mL
½ cup	4 fl. oz.	120 mL
1 cup	8 fl. oz.	240 mL
1 ½ cups	12 fl. oz.	355 mL
2 cups or 1 pint	16 fl. oz.	475 mL
4 cups or 1 quart	32 fl. oz.	1 L
1 gallon	128 fl. oz.	4 L

Oven Temperatures

FAHRENHEIT (F)	CELSIUS (C) (APPROXIMATE)
250°	120°
300°	150°
325°	165°
350°	180°
375°	190°
400°	200°
425°	220°
450°	230°

Volume Equivalents (DRY)

US STANDARD	METRIC (APPROXIMATE)
⅛ teaspoon	0.5 mL
¼ teaspoon	1 mL
½ teaspoon	2 mL
¾ teaspoon	4 mL
1 teaspoon	5 mL
1 tablespoon	15 mL
¼ cup	59 mL
⅓ cup	79 mL
½ cup	118 mL
⅔ cup	156 mL
¾ cup	177 mL
1 cup	235 mL
2 cups or 1 pint	475 mL
3 cups	700 mL
4 cups or 1 quart	1 L

Weight Equivalents

US STANDARD	METRIC (APPROXIMATE)
½ ounce	15 g
1 ounce	30 g
2 ounces	60 g
4 ounces	115 g
8 ounces	225 g
12 ounces	340 g
16 ounces or 1 pound	455 g

INDEX

....

foodie doodles!

Color the frosting on the doughnuts!

Decorate the cupcakes!

Add candles to the birthday cake
and color it in!

Decorate the cookies!

ACKNOWLEDGMENTS

Thank you so much to the readers of Foodlets.com. Our mini foodies in the making are becoming bakers, too! I couldn't have written these recipes without your help testing every single one.

To Lori Kirsten and Leigh Fickling, you're the worst-paid VPs in the history of media and the most supportive friends I could ask for. Thank you to Andrea Sterling for whipping up recipe after recipe (sometimes on a moment's notice) and always offering thoughtful feedback.

To our Supper Club and your kids who tried almost all the recipes here, I adore you: Gina and Mark Rhoades, Beth and Chris Lundberg, Andrea and Terry Sterling, Leigh and Jimmy Fickling.

To the editorial team at Callisto Media, thank you for a dream come true.

To my mother-in-law, Charlene, thank you for always sharing your tried-and-true recipes with me. I've learned so much about baking from you.

To Violet, George, and Estelle, this book was made just for kids between the ages of four through eight and that's you. Phoebe, thank you for testing everything anyway. You're all my favorite bakers forever.

ABOUT THE AUTHOR

Charity Mathews is the author of *Super Simple Baking for Kids* and a former executive at HGTV.com and MarthaStewart.com who's now a family food writer, speaker, and contributor to Food Network and ABC-11. She's also the founder of Foodlets.com, a website full of short-cut recipes packed with fresh ingredients for busy families. Every idea is tested by real kids and designed to encourage a love of good food for a lifetime.

She lives in North Carolina with her husband and four kids on a small farm. They currently share their home with two lab rescues, one bunny, 10 chickens, and 100,000 honey bees.

discover more in the
kid chef
series

Kid Chef Junior
My First Kids' Cookbook
Anjali Shah
978-1-64152-135-2
$14.99 US / $19.99 CAN

Kid Chef
The Foodie Kids' Cookbook:
Healthy Recipes and Culinary
Skills for the New Cook
in the Kitchen
Melina Hammer
978-1-94345-120-3
$15.99 US / $19.99 CAN

Kid Chef Bakes
The Kids' Cookbook
for Aspiring Bakers
Lisa Huff
978-1-62315-942-9
$14.99 US / $19.99 CAN

Kid Chef Every Day
The Easy Cookbook
for Foodie Kids: Simple
Recipes and Essential
Techniques to Wow
Your Family
Colleen Kennedy
978-1-64152-222-9
$16.99 US / $22.99 CAN

 ROCKRIDGE PRESS

Available wherever books and ebooks are sold

CPSIA information can be obtained
at www.ICGtesting.com
Printed in the USA
BVHW021331291119
565196BV00011B/160/P